Also by Kyle L. White

Wisconsin River of Grace

Neighbor As Yourself: Midwest Essays, Poems, Etc.

Winter is Scissors

Haiti! Up!

bear. with me.
{a field journal}

bear. with me.
{a field journal}
kyle l. white

Nazim Hikmet, excerpt from "On Ibrahim Balaban's Painting 'Spring',"
translated by Randy Blasing and Mutlu Konuk,
From Poems of Nazim Hikmet. Copyright 1994, 2002
by Randy Blasing and Mutlu Konuk.
Reprinted by permission of Persea Books, Inc (New York),
www.perseabooks.com. All rights reserved.

ISBN: 9781090845689

"Haven't you ever thought of living
unconsciously like bears, sniffing the earth,
close to pears and the mossy dark,
far from human voices and fire?"
-Nazim Hikmet

Taster of salmon.

Sniffer of cedar and earth.

"Swinger of birches".

-klw

For you.

fig. 1

1.

Call it winter nap,

hibernation, or torpor.

Just don't wake me up.

2.

I'm busy sleeping

five, six, seven months this year.

I could do...July?

3.

"Wake up. Hey! Wake up!

Hibernation is over!"

"Just five more weeks? Please?"

4.

Wake to knotted back.

Tossing, turning from: rocks; roots;

bear snoring. (Me?! No.)

5.

Sky getting lighter.

Finally back to sun's warmth.

But naps end, sadly.

6.

Winter cracks and breaks.

Trillium awakens spring.

Possibilities.

fig. 3

7.

Spring robins calling:
Cheerily, cheer up, cheer up.
Preaching, exhorting.

8.

Lichen covered rocks.

Lake, birch, cedar, meadow, sky.

Kitchen, bedroom, den.

9.

Sniff. Coffee, pipe smoke.

Lake, campfire. Sniff. Pan, walleye.

Sniff. Free fish fry. Sniff.

10.

Banging pans, shouting?

I'm getting mixed messages.

You set the buffet.

11.

Bugs, roots, berries, bark.

Hmm, why? What are you having?

I'll stop by later.

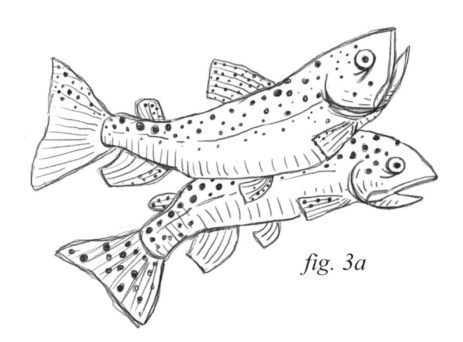

fig. 3a

12.

Speckled. Rainbow. Brown.

Splash about, lil' trout, in the

pan. Lemon, butter.

13.

Scents of distraction:

berries, cedar, miller moths.

Focus on the trout.

14.

Wrap trout in tin foil,

yellow butter and lemon.

Woodfire for fifteen.

15.

Solitude: pipe smoke,

morning prayers, walks, sketchbook,

coffee, toast, butter.

16.

Morning walk log:

Ants, crow, squirrel, worm (deceased),

mourning dove (alone).

fig. 2

k|w.19

17.

Conk-la-ree, chuk-chuk

Chick-a-dee-dee-dee-dee-dee

Hoo-h'HOO-hoo-hoo

18.

Who named the waters?

Names that sound like what they are:

Stream. Lake. River. Pond.

19.

Evening walk log:

Fox, rabbit, moon, clouds, a friend.

Who? The great horned owl.

birch

fig. 4

k/w.19

20.

Moon and Mars ascend

in east, blind to Venus'

west sky jealousy.

21.

Dear Ursa Major,

Who made you, O Great She-Bear?

Pour out your secret.

22.

My roof: Big Dipper.

Me: Urso minor minor.

My bed: moss, rock, earth.

23.

Observe, label it.

Flame. Heat. Water. Steam. But, why

the whistling kettle?

24.

Looking around, down.

I can't make sense of it all,

but for looking up.

fig. 6

klw.19

25.

Burning sun, gold beam.

You silver moon with soft gleam.

All-lay-LU-ee-ya.

26.

Rushing wind so strong.

Clouds sail in heav'n along.

All-lay-LU-ee-ya.

27.

You flowing waters:

Music that the Maker hears.

All-lay-LU-ee-ya.

28.

Lift up your voice! Sing,

creatures of Creator-King,

All-lay-LU-ee-ya.

fig. 7

klw.19

29.

I'm walking these woods.

Is this not God speaking now?

Maker and made: here.

30.

Ah, nature's beauty.

Let us get back to nature.

(Aren't I nature, too?)

31.

Follow rabbit trail.

You meet Bear in a fur coat.

You find Bear is you.

32.

"I imagined your
house down a path in the woods."
"Oh?" (My mind wanders.)

33.

I fear being found.

Best I look from outside-in.

Will you bear with me?

fig. 8

k|w. 19

34.

I live in the woods.

Go away, but don't leave me.

My geography.

35.

Two layers of fur

to keep out water and cold.

But you can come in.

36.

Cedar, oak, birch, elm.

I'm comforted by deep roots.

It's why I love you.

37.

How many full moons?

How many winter slumbers?

I'm counting down now.

38.

Slowing down again.

Thinking of resolutions.

Oh well. Time to nap.

39.

Winter. Spring. Summer.

Fall back to the beginning.

Dying to living.

40.

Torpor: Rouse to snow's
cold bite; return to slumber;
dream of wake-robin.

fig. 9

klw.19

End Notes:

Epigraphs: 1. Quote from Nazim Hikmet poem; 2. "Swinger of birches" line from "Birches" by Robert Frost, from *Mountain Interval*, 1916. Public domain.

#7: "...We have as many teachers and preachers as there are little birds in the air."-Martin Luther, *Commentary on the Sermon on the Mount*

#17: Red-winged Blackbird, Chickadee, Great Horned Owl

#21: Book of Job chapter 9, verse 9

#25-28: Paraphrase of "All Creatures of Our God and King" hymn, from "Canticle of the Sun" poem by St. Francis of Assisi (circa 1225) and based on Psalm 148. William Henry Draper paraphrased the words and put them to music, somewhere between 1899 and 1919. A paraphrase of a paraphrase, then.

#32: Chris said this to me.

#40: The flower wake-robin is better known as trillium.

Made in the USA
Monee, IL
18 January 2022

89213213R00066